HUMAN RIGHTS ARE CHILDREN'S RIGHTS

A guide to ensuring children and young people's rights are respected

NCB promotes the voices, interests and well-being of all children and young people across every aspect of their lives.

As an umbrella body for the children's sector in England and Northern Ireland, we provide essential information on policy, research and best practice for our members and other partners.

NCB aims to:

➔ challenge disadvantage in childhood
➔ work with children and young people to ensure they are involved in all matters that affect their lives
➔ promote multidisciplinary cross-agency partnerships and good practice
➔ influence government policy through policy development and advocacy
➔ undertake high quality research and work from an evidence-based perspective
➔ disseminate information to all those working with children and young people, and to children and young people themselves.

Published by the National Children's Bureau

National Children's Bureau, 8 Wakley Street, London EC1V 7QE
Tel: 020 7843 6000
Website: www.ncb.org.uk
Registered charity number: 258825

NCB works in partnership with Children in Scotland (www.childreninscotland.org.uk) and Children in Wales (www.childreninwales.org.uk).

ISBN: 978-1-905818-37-2

British Library Cataloguing in Publication Data

A catalogue record for this book is available from the British Library

Designed and typeset by Saxon Graphics Limited, Derby, England

Printed by Redlin Printed Limited, Chelmsford, England

This book is printed on a 75% recovered fibre product with FSC certification. It contains a minimum 75% recovered waste. The pulp used in this product is bleached using both the Elemental Chlorine Free (ECF) and Totally Chlorine Free (TCF) processes.

Contents

Acknowledgements

I would like to thank the following people and organisations who have supported me and contributed to this guide:

→ Young advisors – Ellie Munro, Emrys Green, Taiwo Dan and Naushin Shariff
→ National Children's Bureau – Adriana Byrne, Louisa Cook, Rachel Monaghan and Lisa Payne
→ British Institute of Human Rights – Helen Trivers and Lucy Matthews for their contribution, in particular, to Section 7

Thanks also to:

→ Children's Rights Alliance for England – Tom Burke and Carolyne Willow
→ Liberty – Deirdre Malone and Jago Russell
→ Professor Christina Lyon

Janine Young, Head of Children and Young People's Participation, NCB.

Please note

This guide is not legal advice. If you need advice, Section 9 *Useful contacts and further information* will provide you with contacts for organisations who offer information and advice. The information in this guide is correct at the time of printing in July 2008. If there have been changes in the law since the guide was printed, some information may be incorrect or out of date.

Section 1 Introduction

> **What is in this section?**
> - An introduction to human rights
> - What this guide is for

'Children are not mini-persons with mini-rights,
mini-feelings and mini-human dignity.
They are vulnerable human beings with full rights
which require more, not less protection [than adults]'
(Maud de Boer-Buquicchio, Deputy Secretary General,
Council of Europe, 2005)[1]

Human rights belong to everyone, regardless of how old or how young they may be. Because of this, being aware of these rights can remind individuals of the way in which they should behave to one another; can provide agencies with a framework within which they should develop and deliver services; and when necessary, can offer adults, children and young people an opportunity to present their case to a tribunal or court when they feel their rights have been violated. Human rights place the government and public services – including hospitals, schools and social services – under a duty to treat all of us with fairness, equality, dignity and respect.

Children's rights have equal status to adults' rights. However, often children and young people can struggle to find information about their rights or how to take action if their rights have been violated. We need to make sure that children and young people, and the adults who work on their behalf, are familiar with human rights legislation.

What is in the guide?

This guide is written for people who work with children and young people to provide them with basic information on the Human Rights Act 1998, and the way in which it has been used to protect, promote and put into practice children's human rights.

Although not a legal document, the contents of this guide are based on law, in particular as it applies to England. Its aim is to be clear and practical in order to encourage anyone who works with children and young people to improve their own

---

1   Conference speech by the Deputy Secretary General of the Council of Europe, Berlin, 21 October 2005, 'Raising Children Without Violence' www.coe.int/t/e/SG/SGA/documents/speeches/2005/ZH_21102005_Berlin.asp#TopOfPage

understanding of human rights legislation, and enable them to sit down with those young people and discuss how the Human Rights Act 1998 can help and support them.

The legal definition of children in England and in the United Nations Convention on the Rights of the Child is 0–18 years old. In this guide we use the term *children and young people* to describe this age group.

Please note

If the issues you're concerned about do not seem to relate to any specific articles in the Human Rights Act 1998, it does not mean that you cannot challenge a local authority or service provider to get a child's needs met. Those issues may be covered by other pieces of legislation such as the Children Act 1989, and various health, education or anti-discrimination laws. Information about how to take an issue forward is given in *Section 8*.

The Human Rights Act is broken down into different articles (sections) and in this guide we explain what some of them mean for children and young people. We also refer to actual case studies where human rights have been, or could be, used to improve children and young people's lives.

Section 8 of this guide gives practical advice and information on how you might go about successfully using the Human Rights Act to support children and young people. Using the Act does not necessarily mean going through a court system. It is as much about raising your own awareness of what human rights mean; using that awareness to improve your practice; and communicating that awareness and understanding to the children and young people who you work with. When a human rights violation may require a more formal investigation and response, we will show you what the alternatives are and where to get further information if you want to take an issue further.

Section 2 Background

What is in this section?

- Why we're focusing on the Human Rights Act 1998
- The UN Convention on the Rights of the Child
- Anti-discrimination and equality laws

The **United Nations Convention on the Rights of the Child** (UNCRC) sets out over forty civil, cultural, economic, social and political rights for children and young people from birth to the age of 18. Since its adoption in 1989, it has influenced the lives of children all over the world. Almost all the countries in the world have agreed to respect the same principles underpinning the rights of children. The UK ratified (signed up to) the UN Convention in 1991 and, by doing so, agreed to abide by its requirements, and is obliged to implement its provisions.[2]

At the moment, the UNCRC as a whole is not part of UK domestic law. This means that if a human right contained in the UNCRC has been violated, a child or young person is not able to go to court to seek redress.

However, rights in the UNCRC can be used to support decisions by a court. Also, the UK government is subject to a reporting process: the UN Committee on the Rights of the Child requires the government to report on the implementation of the UNCRC every five years, after which the Committee responds to the government with a list of recommendations to support full implementation.

Children also have human rights contained in the **Human Rights Act 1998**. This is part of UK law so the rights are enforceable. If a child or young person thinks that their rights under the Human Rights Act have been ignored or violated, they can take action to ensure their rights are respected. This means that the Human Rights Act is a powerful tool to protect children's rights (see *Section 4* of this guide).

It is also worth noting that other enforcement measures are available under anti-discrimination legislation, such as the **Equality Act 2006**. This legislation relates to unfair or discriminatory treatment based on a person's age, disability, gender, race,

---

2   Article 26 of the Vienna Convention on the Law of Treaties, 1969, ratified by the UK in 1971, provides that *'Every treaty in force is binding upon the parties to it and must be performed by them in good faith'*.

sexuality, or religion and culture; and it also created the Equality and Human Rights Commission.

Ideally, the child-specific Articles of the UNCRC can be used to complement the Articles of the Human Rights Act and other domestic laws (such as the Children Acts and Employment Equality (Age) Regulations 2006), to protect children's rights and work in their best interests. It can also inform complaints processes, as well as the rare cases that require a hearing before a court (see *Section 7* of this guide for examples).

Section 3 What are human rights?

> **What is in this section?**
> • The basic principles of human rights explained

Human rights are the rights possessed by everyone, by virtue of their common humanity, to live a life of freedom and dignity. They give all people moral claims on how they live and how they are treated. Human rights are universal, inalienable, indivisible and shared.

➜ **Universal**, because they belong to everyone without exception.
➜ **Inalienable**, because it is impossible for anyone to give up their human rights, even if he or she wanted to, since every person is accorded those rights by virtue of being human. In addition, no person or group of persons can take away another individual's human rights.
➜ **Indivisible**, because all of the fundamental human rights are of equal importance and are interrelated. These rights express our deepest commitments to ensuring that everyone has the freedoms and things that are necessary for dignified living.
➜ **Shared**, because everyone has an equal claim to a human right. No one person's human rights are more important than someone else's. Often we will need to find a proportionate balance to implementing human rights so that everyone's dignity is assured (see *Section 5* of this guide).

Human rights are based on a number of basic principles, including Fairness, Respect, Equality and Dignity.[3]

---

3   Butler, F (2007) *Rights for Real: Older people, their human rights and the CEHR.*

Dignity

Human dignity is the basis of all fundamental rights. Treating someone with dignity means treating them in a way that values their inherent worth as a human being.

Equality

All people – children, young people and adults – are of equal worth with entitlement to the full set of human rights and the means to exercise these rights effectively. While this protects people from discriminatory acts or behaviour, it does not mean that everyone should necessarily be treated the same because equal treatment may not be enough to provide equality of opportunity or equal outcomes. An equal society recognises the diverse needs, situations and goals of individuals; removes discrimination and prejudice; and tackles the economic, political, legal, social and physical barriers that limit what people can do and be.

Fairness

A fair society is one that is free from prejudice and discrimination and in which people of all ages are able to achieve their potential and to participate fully in their communities.

Respect

Respect is about how we should treat one another in society. Respect means valuing one another, and taking account of each other's individual needs and desires.

Section 4 What is the Human Rights Act?

> **What is in this section?**
>
> • How the Human Rights Act 1998 was created
>
> • An explanation of how public authorities should support children and young people's needs better through the Human Rights Act

The human rights contained in the Human Rights Act belong to *all individuals* in the UK regardless of their age, nationality and citizenship. They are fundamentally important in maintaining a fair and civilised society. They also underpin and complement anti-discrimination and equality laws like the Disability Discrimination Act 1995 or the Equality Act 2006.

The Human Rights Act 1998:

➡ incorporates most of the human rights contained in the European Convention on Human Rights into UK law

➡ tells the courts in the UK that judges should interpret all laws in a way that is compatible with human rights

➡ requires the government to ensure that the law is compatible with human rights obligations

➡ tells public authorities that they must act in a way that is compatible with human rights

➡ enables anyone who thinks their rights have been breached by a public authority to bring a claim against that authority in UK courts or via a range of other systems and processes, including complaints procedures and tribunals, as appropriate.

This has made a huge difference to many people's lives. The Human Rights Act is a practical tool that can, through human rights advocacy, support and empower individuals who are providing a service to children and young people – as well as to the children and young people themselves, if they feel they are facing discrimination, disadvantage or exclusion.

It also means that children and young people, and those working on their behalf, have the power to tackle inequality by themselves promoting children's human rights; and, when necessary, challenge instances where a child's or young person's human rights may have been ignored or violated.

The Convention for the Protection of Human Rights and Fundamental Freedoms commonly known as the **European Convention on Human Rights** (**ECHR**) is a binding international agreement drafted in post-war Europe, and ratified by the UK government in 1951. It enshrines fundamental civil and political rights but until its incorporation into UK law, in 1998, could only be contested in the European Court of Human Rights in Strasbourg. Taking forward a human rights case could prove a time-consuming and expensive process for individuals.

The Human Rights Act came into force in 2000. Since then people in the UK can claim their ECHR rights by going to the UK courts; because the Human Rights Act 1998 made most of the ECHR part of our UK law. It is now much quicker and simpler for individuals to take their cases to court to claim their rights. As a last resort, you can still take your case to the European Court of Human Rights if you do not agree with the outcome of your case in the UK courts.

As significant, however, is the way in which having a human rights law in place contributes to a change in our culture: in particular, the way in which people, including children and young people, are beginning to address unfair practice and challenge public services/authorities that fail to treat them with fairness, dignity and respect. There are examples in *Section 7* of where this has happened successfully, as well as some that have not been so successful.

What are the responsibilities of public authorities?

What are public authorities?

Public authorities are the organisations that carry out a governmental or public function. Examples are departments of central government (e.g. the Department for Children, Schools and Families which oversees early years and school-age education as well as many child policy areas); local authorities (including social services); state-maintained schools; the police; immigration services; prison services; and the National Health Service (NHS). There are some circumstances where private sector organisations that are delivering public services may be considered to be public authorities, such as private prisons (for more information, see the box below). When you think about it, children have to deal with a lot of these public authorities every day – every time they meet a police officer, go to the doctor or go to school, they are in a relationship with a 'public authority'.

Human rights provide us with minimum standards that public authorities must not go below – fixed standards against which to judge unfair treatment.

Children and young people should be able to expect that:

→ public authorities respect their human rights, as these rights form a common set of binding values for public authorities right across the UK

→ public authorities have the Human Rights Act in mind when they make decisions that impact on children and young people's rights

→ human rights are considered by public authorities throughout policy and practice.

It is important to understand that our human rights as recognised by the Human Rights Act can only be enforced against public authorities, such as the government, local authorities, state schools and hospitals. There is a lack of agreement over whether 'public authorities' include private sector organisations that deliver a public service, like private care homes.

Articles in the Human Rights Act have been used as a standard to challenge poor treatment and negotiate improvements to services provided by public authorities. Public authorities should be encouraged to put fundamental ideas like fairness, dignity and respect at the heart of their services and actions; and must behave in a non-discriminatory way that supports equality of treatment.

Section 5 Balancing rights

What is in this section?
- Balancing your rights against other people's rights
- How the different articles in the Human Rights Act are grouped

The Human Rights Act 1998 is about identifying, recognising and respecting everyone's rights. All of the rights are vital to a healthy democracy and to individual respect, but not all of the articles that comprise the ECHR and Human Rights Act carry the same weight – especially if there is a real and serious danger to public safety.

This means that one individual's rights will often have to be balanced against another person's rights. For example, your right to express your views publicly may need to be balanced against another person's right to a private life. Or for example, the rights of a person accused of a crime to question witnesses may need to be balanced against the rights of the victims and vulnerable witnesses. However, some rights are so fundamental that they can never be interfered with, not even in times of war or national emergency.

The whole system of respecting rights works best when people act responsibly and with respect towards others and the wider community.

The different articles in the Human Rights Act can be grouped into three broad types: absolute, limited, and qualified rights.

➔ **Absolute rights** – these can never be withheld or taken away, such as the right not to be subject to torture or inhumane and degrading treatment or punishment (Article 3).
Other rights can be interfered with in some circumstances, so can be considered to be limited rights and qualified rights.

➔ **Limited rights** – these may be limited under specific circumstances. For example, the right to liberty (Article 5) can be limited if you are convicted of a criminal offence and sent to serve a custodial sentence.

➔ **Qualified rights** – these are rights that require a balance between the rights of you as an individual and the needs of the wider community or state interest. They can only be interfered with if this is absolutely necessary and proportionate. A *proportionate interference* is one that is appropriate and not excessive in the circumstances. For example, your right to freedom of expression can be restricted if you are inciting racial hatred, which is prohibited by law.

Qualified rights include the right to respect for private and family life (Article 8); the right to practise your own religion or beliefs (Article 9); freedom of expression (Article 10); and freedom of assembly and association (Article 11).

Please note

If you are unsure whether a situation led to unfair treatment or a clear violation of an article in the Act, consider seeking legal advice. There is advice on where you can get support in *Section 8* of this guide.

Section 6 What is in the Human Rights Act 1998?

What is in this section?

- What the Human Rights Act covers
- What articles and protocols are included in the Act

There are 16 rights in the Human Rights Act, made up of articles and protocols.[4] These articles and protocols involve matters of life and death, like the freedom from torture and being killed; but also cover rights in everyday life, such as what a person can say and do, their beliefs, their right to an education and what we would now consider 'other entitlements'.

---

4   A protocol, in this instance, is a later addition to the ECHR, which is the source of the Human Rights Act.

The articles are listed below in their simplest form.

Article 1:   *Article 1 does not appear in the Human Rights Act. It appears in the European Convention on Human Rights. It means that the UK has promised everyone in the UK the rights and freedoms that are contained in the Convention.*

Article 2:   **the right to life protected by the law**

Article 3:   **the right not to be tortured or treated in an inhuman or degrading way**

Article 4:   **the right to be free from slavery or forced labour**

Article 5:   **the right to liberty**

Article 6:   **the right to a fair trial and public hearing**

Article 7:   **the right to no punishment without the law**

Article 8:   **the right to respect for private and family life, home and correspondence**

Article 9:   **the right to freedom of thought, conscience and religion**

Article 10:   **the right to freedom of expression**

Article 11:   **the right to free assembly and association**

Article 12:   **the right to marry and found a family**

Article 13:   *this article also doesn't appear in the Human Rights Act either. It would offer the 'right to an effective remedy', but the Human Rights Act itself is seen as fulfilling that promise.*

Article 14:   **the right not to be discriminated against** in relation to the other rights contained in the Human Rights Act

Protocol 1, Article 1:   **the right to peaceful enjoyment of possessions**

Protocol 1, Article 2:   **the right to education**

Protocol 1, Article 3:   **the right to free elections**

Protocol 13, Article 1:   **the abolition of the death penalty**

Section 7 Examples of children and young people's claims to human rights

---

What is in this section?

• Further information about some of the human rights, contained in the Human Rights Act, that are most relevant to children and young people

• Actual case studies of where children and young people, and those working on their behalf, have used the Human Rights Act to challenge poor treatment or improve lives

---

The Human Rights Act is a very useful tool in promoting, supporting and enforcing children's rights in the UK. This section of the guide provides a range of examples of where human rights have been, or could be, used to improve children and young people's lives. This includes cases taken to an ombudsman,[5] tribunal or court, and also cases where people have simply used human rights language outside any formal procedure in order to challenge poor or unfair treatment. Even if not always successful, these cases can have a beneficial effect on all children and young people because they identify a failure in practice that needs to be addressed and corrected, not only by the agencies responsible for the alleged violation but also through a change in government policy and official guidance.

All of the rights contained in the Human Rights Act belong to, and are relevant for, children and young people. However some rights have been used more often and relate more specifically to the particular issues that children or young people may face in their lives. Before giving examples of cases where human rights have or could be used, the table below provides more details about some of the most relevant rights for children. This will help you understand how they have been used in the cases that follow, and help you determine whether any of the issues you are facing or working with involve these particular human rights.

---

5   An ombudsman plays an official role in carrying out independent investigations into complaints about public services. See *Section 9* for information on Local Government Ombudsman and Parliamentary and Health Service Ombudsman.

Right	Some relevant issues
Article 3: the right not to be tortured or treated in an inhuman or degrading way Everyone, including every child, has the right not to be tortured or treated in an inhuman or degrading way. This right is an absolute right, which means that no one can ever be tortured or treated in an inhuman or degrading way, under any circumstances. Only the most serious kinds of ill treatment will be covered by this right. Inhuman treatment means treatment causing severe mental or physical harm. Degrading treatment means treatment that is grossly humiliating and undignified. Inhuman or degrading treatment does not have to be deliberate – it is the impact it has which matters.	Child abuse or neglect Severe bullying Poor and/or abusive treatment while in institutional care/custody Excessive restraint while in custody Poor conditions in institutions or in custody
Article 6: the right to a fair trial and public hearing The right to a fair trial contains a number of principles that need to be considered at some stage in decision-making processes regarding criminal charges or 'civil rights and obligations'. The person whose rights are being affected has a right to all of the following: ➜ an independent and impartial tribunal ➜ be present at some stage during the decision-making process (although this can be restricted) ➜ have an opportunity to present their case before the decision is made ➜ an adversarial hearing – which means that they can say and know what others have said, challenge any inaccuracies that exist through cross-examination and address the decision-making panel themselves ➜ disclosure of all relevant documents ➜ have their hearing take place within a reasonable time – the phrase 'reasonable time' may mean different things to decision-makers and those whose rights are affected ➜ be given reasons that will help them to understand the decision that has been made. This right applies most obviously to court proceedings (e.g. criminal trials), but the principles must also be considered in a number of other processes including tribunal cases, school exclusions and childcare proceedings such as adoption and fostering.	Proceedings that do not cater for the needs of children, e.g. dealing with young offenders in adult courts Failure to provide children with an opportunity to present their views Failure to protect the privacy of children during proceedings

Article 8: the right to respect for private and family life, home and correspondence

This right is a very wide-ranging right. It protects four interests: family life, private life, home, and correspondence.

→ **Family life** is interpreted broadly. It is not restricted to blood relationships, and includes close and personal ties of a family kind.

→ **Private life** is also interpreted broadly. It includes issues such as making choices about how you live your life; participating in decisions about your life; privacy; relationships; physical and mental well-being; and access to personal information.

→ The right to respect for **home** is not a right to housing, but a right to respect for the home someone already has.

→ **Correspondence** covers all forms of communication, including phone calls, letters, faxes and emails.

This right is a **qualified right**. It may be interfered with in order to take account of the rights of other individuals and/or the wider community. Any interference with this right must be necessary and **proportionate** (see page 14).

Separation of families, e.g. in child care proceedings, immigration decisions

Denying young people access to public areas

Access to personal information and confidentiality

Invasions of privacy, e.g. fingerprinting, body searches, use of CCTV

Abuse or mistreatment of children

Children not being able to participate in important decisions about their lives

Article 9: the right to freedom of thought, conscience and religion

This right contains two aspects. The freedom to hold and change a religion or a belief is an absolute right which cannot be qualified in any way. The state cannot legislate as to how people should think.

However, there are limitations on the freedom to *manifest* a religion or belief, through worship, teaching, practice and observance. This part of the right is a qualified right. It may be interfered with or restricted in order to take account of the rights of other individuals and/or the wider community. Any interference must be necessary and **proportionate** (see page 14).

Religious/cultural clothing incorporated into school uniforms

Religious/cultural practices (e.g. praying) during school hours

Article 14: the right not to be discriminated against in relation to the other rights contained in the Human Rights Act

Discrimination takes place where someone is treated in a different way to someone else in a similar situation. Discrimination also includes treating people with very different needs in the same way. Differential treatment will not be discrimination, however, if it can be shown to be 'objectively and reasonably' justified.

This right does not protect against discrimination in all circumstances – it must be used alongside another right contained in the Human Rights Act. For example, if a disabled child is unable to go on a school trip because they are not provided with adequate support, this may breach the right not to be discriminated against alongside the right to respect for private life.

Discrimination is prohibited on a non-exhaustive list of grounds including 'sex, race, colour, language, religion, political or other opinion, national or social origin, association with a national minority, property, birth or other status'. 'Other status' would include discrimination on the basis of age – children must not be discriminated against because of their age, or for any other reason.

Young people not being allowed to access certain areas, e.g. shopping malls

Discriminatory school admission policies

Discrimination faced by particular groups, e.g. disabled children, asylum seeker children, Gypsy and Traveller children, children from a particular religion

Protocol 1, Article 2: the right to education

This right says that no person shall be denied the right to education. This does not mean that a pupil has a right to learn what they want, wherever they want – the right to education entails:

➜ a right of access to educational facilities that exist
➜ a right to an 'effective' education
➜ a right to have completed programmes of study officially recognised.

Parents' beliefs (e.g. religion) must be considered in the way schools are allocated by local authorities. The UK government has entered a 'special reservation' in this area, saying that the rights of parents should only be respected in so far as this is compatible with efficient education and the avoidance of unreasonable public expenditure.

Education of children with special educational needs (SEN)

Access to education for children who are seriously ill

Access to education for children in custody

Bullying

Issues and cases

In the remainder of this section of the guide is a range of examples illustrating where human rights have been, or could be, used to improve children or young people's lives. They are grouped loosely under four main headings – protection of children, discrimination, basic needs, and decision-making. We have chosen these particular issues either because they are examples of how human rights legislation has been used to challenge the particular issues, or because they are issues which are, in our experience, particularly relevant to children and young people in the UK.

Remember, however, that these are just some of the key issues facing children and young people today in the UK. There are a range of other issues where human rights may be relevant and it is not possible to cover all of them in this guide. If you are unsure whether an issue you are dealing with is a human rights issue, you can contact one of the organisations listed in *Section 9* for further advice.

Protecting children

Mistreatment of children

Children and young people sometimes suffer horrific abuse and mistreatment, while in the care of the state or while at home. Abuse of children may be covered by other legislation, including the Children Acts and criminal law. However it is important to recognise that this is also a human rights issue. Child abuse or mistreatment, whether physical or psychological, will have an impact on a child's physical and/or psychological well-being, and therefore on their right to respect for private life (Article 8). In serious cases this may also be inhuman or degrading treatment (Article 3).

Instances of abuse and other forms of mistreatment that take place while in state care may therefore be a breach of the right to respect for private life and/or the right not to be treated in an inhuman or degrading way. Examples of this may be abuse of asylum seeker children in detention centres or excessive restraint techniques used on children while in custody.

Some children and young people may face extremely poor living conditions in state care – such as in young offenders' institutions, temporary accommodation or children's homes – including overcrowding, lack of privacy or inadequate sanitary facilities. This may also interfere with their right to respect for private life, or in extreme conditions may be inhuman or degrading treatment.

Public authorities such as social services must take positive steps to protect children and young people from inhuman or degrading treatment, even if the harm is carried out by private individuals rather than directly by the public authority. If, for example, social services are made aware of evidence that a child is being abused at home they may have a duty under the Human Rights Act to investigate or intervene.

Case example 1

Four children were subject to gross neglect and maltreatment over a five-year period, with the result that they were never properly fed, lived in unsanitary conditions and were subject to physical abuse. This had devastating and long-lasting effects on their physical and psychological health. This was found to have been a violation of Article 3 (the right not to be treated in an inhuman or degrading way) because the authorities had been aware of the serious ill-treatment over a period of years and failed to take action to protect the children. While the local authorities were initially justified in maintaining the family as a unit by giving support to the parents, the gravity of the conditions and the signs that the children were suffering physical and psychological damage required that effective steps be taken to safeguard their welfare.

Case reference: *Z and others v UK (2001)*

Bullying

Bullying can be a very serious issue for some children – and can have a huge impact on their right to respect for private life. In extreme cases bullying may also amount to inhuman or degrading treatment. If a child stops going to school because they are being bullied, this will also impact on their right to education (Protocol 1, Article 2).

State schools (and other public authorities) that are aware that bullying is taking place may have a positive duty under the Human Rights Act to take action. If schools fail to protect a child or young person from bullying, this failure to act may be a breach of their right to respect for private life, or their right not to be treated in an inhuman or degrading way.

Invasions of privacy

The right to respect for private life places limits on the extent to which a public authority can do things which invade your privacy or physical integrity without your permission. Some schools carry out activities such as body searches, drug testing, fingerprinting and surveillance in classrooms. These kinds of activities could breach the right to respect for private life – particularly if they are carried out on all children and young people regardless of whether there is any reason to suspect them of having done anything wrong.

It is important to remember, however, that the right to respect for private life is a qualified right. This means that this right can be interfered with in order to protect the rights of others and the wider interests of the community – including the safety of children and staff in school. However, any interference with this right must be **proportionate** and not excessive (see page 14). If you feel that schools – or any other public authorities – are invading the privacy of children or young people in a way that is disproportionate to the situation, you may be able to challenge this using the right to respect for private life.

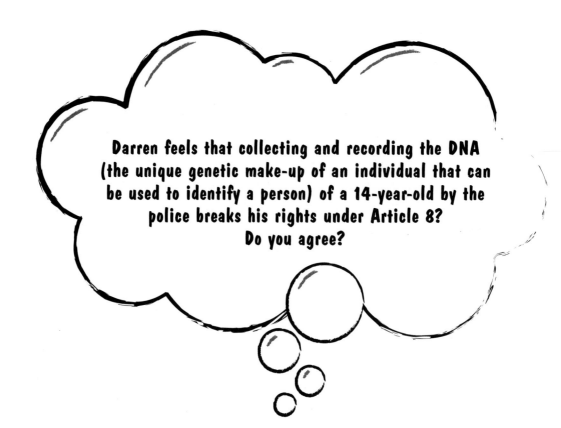

Darren feels that collecting and recording the DNA (the unique genetic make-up of an individual that can be used to identify a person) of a 14-year-old by the police breaks his rights under Article 8? Do you agree?

Sharing personal information

The right to respect for private life includes the right to have personal information – such as official records, photographs, letters, diaries and medical information – kept private and confidential. Unless there is a very good reason, public authorities should not collect or use information like this. Any disclosure of personal information must be necessary and **proportionate**, as the right to respect for private life is a qualified right (see page 14).

Children should also be able to access information that is held about them by public authorities. If public authorities decide to withhold information, there needs to be a legitimate reason for doing so, such as if releasing the information could cause significant harm to the child or someone else. Again, this reason must be necessary and proportionate.

Case example 2

A young man wanted access to his personal file held by the local authority. He had been in care from a young age and wanted to find out about his past. The local authority refused. This was found to breach his right to respect for his private life. People should have access to information about themselves unless there is a specific justification for withholding the information.

Case reference: *Gaskin v UK (1999)*

As part of the development of a national information-sharing database, called ContactPoint, the government plans to gather, record and share basic identifying information on all children and young people in England. This will include the sharing of information about school children between local authority professionals such as in schools, social services and the police.

> **But what information should be shared, and who should decide if it's kept and whether it's shared? Tanya believes that if a young person visits a 'sensitive service' (including those providing advice on drugs, alcohol and family planning) these details should not be stored for other professionals to access. Do you agree?**

Discrimination

Children and young people often face discrimination in their daily lives, simply because of their age. Media coverage of children and young people is often negative, which in turn exacerbates discrimination against them. Some groups of children and young people will be particularly vulnerable to discrimination; for example disabled children and young people, or those belonging to Gypsy and Traveller communities. Here we outline some areas where the right not to be discriminated against (Article 14) has or could be used to challenge discrimination. However, there are a wide range of circumstances in which children and young people may face discrimination, in addition to the issues we have included here.

Remember that the right not to be discriminated against is not a freestanding right. If you want to use this right in order to challenge discrimination, you need to use it alongside another right in the Human Rights Act.

Denying children and young people access to public areas

Children and young people may sometimes be denied access to public areas; through curfews, for example, or 'dispersal zones' that enable police to remove young people from certain areas at certain times (see Case example 3). Another example is the 'mosquito device' which is designed to deter young people from hanging around, usually near retail premises or businesses, by emitting a high-pitched noise that causes discomfort to their ears. The frequency of the device is above the hearing range of people over 25.

These kinds of actions are likely to have an impact on young people's right to respect for their private life (Article 8). Therefore they could be argued to be discriminatory under Article 14, alongside the right to respect for private life, as they only apply to children.

The human rights organisation, Liberty, has case studies of groups of young people in Corby and in Middlesbrough who have led campaigns against the Mosquito and convinced local councils to ban their use by public authorities. Liberty's contact details appear in *Section 9*.

Case example 3

A dispersal zone was created by the police in Richmond, giving police the power to take home anyone under 16 who was in the 'dispersal zone' after 9pm without an adult. This was challenged by a 14-year-old boy who didn't want to be taken home in a police car so felt that he couldn't go out after 9pm – even to the shops to buy some milk or to return home from his band practice. He thought this 'curfew' was not fair because it was indiscriminate and he had done nothing wrong.

The human rights organisation, Liberty, helped the boy with his case. They told the court that the police's curfew power interfered with the boy's right to respect for his private and family life (Article 8), including the ability to associate with his friends and to engage in activities with them. The UK Court of Appeal accepted that it would be wrong for the police to pick up young people who had done nothing wrong. The Court ruled that the power only applied to under-16s who were behaving badly or who were at risk of harm.

Case reference: *W v Richmond-upon-Thames [2006]*

Religious freedom in schools

Schools often place restrictions on religious clothing or jewellery in school uniforms. Restrictions on religious clothing or jewellery will interfere with the right to freedom of thought, conscience and religion (Article 9) and may also be considered to be discriminatory (Article 14). However, as the right to manifest your religious beliefs under Article 9 is a qualified right, it can be balanced against the rights of others or the wider community. Although not always successful, there have been a number of cases where students have used the Human Rights Act to challenge this kind of restriction – including the case below which is currently before the courts.

Other aspects of religious freedom in schools include provision of prayer facilities where children wish to pray during the day; and ensuring culturally sensitive food is available at school canteens, such as halal food. If a school prevents children from manifesting their religious beliefs through worship, practice and observance, they need to be able to justify this as being necessary and proportionate. Children also have a right to religious views that differ from those of the school, and must not be discriminated against for their beliefs.

Case example 4

On 29 July 2008 the High Court ruled that 14-year-old Sarika Singh was a victim of unlawful discrimination. She was excluded from her school for wearing a Sikh religious bangle. The Kara (the Sikh bangle) has racial and religious significance to her.

Sarika Singh was forced to have school lessons in isolation from her peers for two months and had been excluded from the school in South Wales since 5 November 2007. The human rights group, Liberty, represented her and successfully argued that the Aberdare Girls' School had breached race relations and human rights laws by excluding her. The ruling also upheld a 25-year-old Law Lords' decision which allows Sikh children to wear items representing their faith, including turbans, to school. Please visit Liberty's website (see *Section 9* of this guide) for more details.

Discrimination faced by vulnerable groups

It is important to remember that children may also face discrimination for other reasons alongside that of their age. Some groups of children are particularly vulnerable to discrimination, for example asylum-seeking children, children in care, children in conflict with the law, disabled children, Gypsy and Traveller children, and young carers.

The Human Rights Act applies to everyone equally in the UK, regardless of their status – including whether they are citizens – and therefore provides these groups with an important form of protection. These groups face a wide range of issues, including discrimination. Many of these issues are touched on in this guide but it is beyond its scope to explore the issues facing particular groups in detail. If there are specific issues you have concerns about, please refer to *Section 8* of this guide.

Basic needs

Family life

The right to respect for family life includes being able to live together as a family, and, where this is not possible, having regular contact. This right becomes particularly relevant for children when there is a possibility they may be taken into care, or if their parents are being imprisoned or detained under mental health legislation. It is also very relevant for children in custody who are separated from their families. Restrictions placed on family visits for children who are in custody will have an impact on their right to respect for family life.

When restrictions are placed on family life, public authorities should consider whether separating the family is necessary, and whether there are any less-restrictive options which would allow the family to remain living together or to have the maximum level of contact.

In some circumstances it will be necessary to separate a family, in order to protect the child. Social services and other public authorities have a duty to protect children from being treated in an inhuman or degrading way (Article 3), or in extreme cases the right to life (Article 2). If a child is taken into care it is important that the procedures follow the principles of the right to a fair trial (Article 6) and their right to respect for their private and family life (Article 8).

Case example 5

A woman with mental health problems struggled following the death of her husband. She was placed in 24-hour supported care and her children were fostered. It was agreed that the children could visit their mother three times a week but these visits were gradually reduced to one a week on the basis that the authority did not have enough staff to supervise them. The mother's advocate referred to the children's right to respect for a family life (Article 8) to challenge this service failure and as a result the three visits a week were restored.

Source: *The Human Rights Act: Changing Lives (2007)*
British Institute of Human Rights (BIHR).

Access to education

As mentioned above, the right to education does not include a right to be educated however you want, wherever you want. However, it does include a right to access the existing education system. This will be particularly relevant for children for whom education is hard to access – for example children who are in hospital for long periods of time, or children who are in custody. If children in these kinds of situations are unable to access the existing educational system, this may breach their right to education.

The right to education is also relevant when children with special educational needs do not have their assessed needs met – see Case example 6. Failure to meet assessed needs may breach the right to education if this prevents a child from effectively accessing education (Protocol 1, Article 2). If discrimination is involved in not meeting these needs, this may also breach the right not to be discriminated against (Article 14).

Case example 6

Michael has Down's syndrome. According to his statement of special educational needs, speech and language therapy was supposed to be provided for him, as well as other kinds of help. Michael's therapist retired, and there was a long delay in finding a replacement. This meant that Michael did not get the help he needed from a speech and language therapist for a year.

Because speech and language therapy was part of the special educational provision set out in Michael's statement, the council had a duty to make sure Michael received it after his therapist retired. The Local Government Ombudsman (LGO) found that this breached the right to education under the Human Rights Act. The council accepted this and, on the LGO's recommendation, agreed to make payments to Michael and his mother to buy the extra help needed to help Michael catch up on the speech and language therapy he had missed.

Source: *Local Government Ombudsman Case reference 02/B/17184*

Decision-making procedures

Being involved in decision-making

Participation is an important aspect of human rights. Children have a right to have their views and opinions taken into account when decisions that affect them are made. Article 12 of the UN Convention on the Rights of the Child gives children the right to express their views in decisions that affect them, and to have their views taken into account (in accordance with their age and maturity). While the Human Rights Act does not contain a specific right to participate and be involved in decisions, participation is an important underpinning principle. The right to respect for private life (Article 8) places emphasis on the importance of being able to participate in decisions about your life.

The UNCRC and the Human Rights Act can be used to support the involvement of young people in decisions through mechanisms such as student councils in schools and government consultations with young people over legislation that directly affects them. They can also be used to support young people to have their views heard during court proceedings and in decisions about their lives; for example school admissions and exclusions, and care proceedings.

Case example 7

Three teenage boys wanted to be represented separately in court by their own solicitor, in order to represent their views on who they should live with following their parents' separation. They used their right to respect for their private and family life (and also referred to Article 12 of the Convention of the Rights of the Child) to successfully uphold their right to independent representation and therefore their right to have their opinions listened to in court.

Case reference: *Mabon v Mabon [2005]*

Fairness in decision-making

Another very important right to consider in decision-making procedures that affect children is the right to a fair trial. The principles of a fair trial (see page 19) must be followed in court proceedings involving children, and in other processes such as care proceedings. In particular, children have a right to have their views and opinions heard and to be provided with adequate support and representation.

It is important to remember that what is considered to be a 'fair trial' for adults may not be a fair trial for children. Children may have particular needs, and the right to a fair trial takes this into account. For example, in the case of trials involving children, the right to a fair trial allows for the exclusion of the press or public in order to protect the interests of the young person.

Section 8 Practical advice and information: What can you do next?

What is in this section?

- Different routes that don't always end up in court
- Some practical ideas of how to take your issues forward
- How to get advice on your rights
- Who the experts are who could help you
- Where to go for legal advice

Anyone who feels that a public authority has failed to respect a child or young person's human rights can raise this with the service provider (such as the school or hospital) or the local authority (for example the councillors) by making a public complaint, going to an Ombudsman, or taking it to an appropriate UK court or tribunal. The route you choose to follow depends on a number of factors: the nature of the potential violation of rights, the individual circumstances of the case, and the type of response that would lead to a timely and satisfactory conclusion for the child or young person. It's helpful to get advice from one of the organisations listed in *Section 9* before deciding what action to take.

What are your options?

Many people think that the only way to get a child or young person's rights upheld is to go to court. This is an important option, but not always necessary. The diagram (below) sets out the different ways that people can ensure their rights are upheld.

Service providers and public authorities are required to have complaints procedures in place, and should make information available explaining how to pursue a complaint. It can begin with an informal complaint to the service provider, leading to a more formal, written complaint where necessary. If the complainant is unhappy with the outcome of that process, they can take the complaint to the local or other public authority that is responsible for commissioning that service or is accountable for the quality of the service provided. If that decision still leaves the complainant feeling dissatisfied and it involves a local authority service, they can take a case to the Local Government Ombudsman.

Lowest number of cases

The European Court of Human Rights

Going through the British Courts

Utilising the local ombudsman

Using more formal internal complaints procedures

Starting with simple steps, for example speaking or writing to the right person in the service or local authority

Highest number of cases

Taking a case to tribunal or court is normally – but does not have to be – the final stage. An individual who feels that their rights have been violated can decide to take the case to court and bypass the other stages outlined above. Under the Human Rights Act, if the person disagrees with the court's decision and has pursued the issue as far as it can go in the UK, he or she may take the case to the European Court of Human Rights.

Pursuing a human rights complaint can be a daunting proposition, but there are people available to help (see *Section 9*). Specialist organisations have advisors on hand who can offer guidance and help you clarify what issues may be involved and what opportunities there might be to help resolve the issue. Advocates are available to listen and talk through the issue, provide advice and support, help you formulate the child's complaint and present their problem and, if you wish, represent the child or young person either in writing or in a meeting.

Case studies 5 and 6 in *Section 7* give examples of cases that did not go to court.

How to get advice on your rights

There are a number of organisations with experts who have worked with children and young people in the past and can guide you in taking a complaint forward:

→ Liberty
→ The Children's Legal Centre
→ Children's Rights Alliance for England (CRAE)
→ Equality and Human Rights Commission.

Further details of these organisations and other useful support can be found in *Section 9*. It is important to be prepared with accurate information about the issue when you approach an organisation for help and advice. It would be helpful to be clear about the facts of the case you're concerned about, and to make notes of what happened before making contact with them.

Many of the organisations listed in this guide have information services that you can access. If you have access to the internet, look on their websites to see what information they have that may be of use to you to save you time.

Some support services may ask for a 'query form' to be completed online or a letter to be sent in to explain the issue. They should give you step-by-step information on the best way to contact them and what information they require in order to answer your questions, as well as an indication of how long it might take them to get back to you.

Other support services offer a telephone service so that you, or the child or young person you represent, can talk to an advisor who will try to clarify the facts of your case and help you understand whether and which human rights issues should be considered.

How could these experts help?

Some services can only provide information but others offer advice and can sometimes point you in the direction of getting more support if you need it. For example, adult advocates can work through the issue with you and the child you are trying to help.

The experts can give you both practical ideas on how to carry an issue forward and highlight which human rights areas may have been violated. They may be able to predict what the response is likely to be from the person you will complain to; and how you could respond to it. They can also advise you when you may not have a clear human rights case, but do have grounds for complaint about a service failure.

Although some of these organisations offer legal advice, they do not always have the resources to take on individual cases but can refer you to other organisations that may be able to do so. They can also help you to work with the child or young person to organise the information about the case in a way that will be most helpful to a solicitor.

Questions you may want to ask the experts once you have told them about your issue

Once you have collected all the facts, you may want to ask them the following questions:

→ What are the child's rights in this area?
→ Do you think we may have a legitimate complaint?
→ Do you think that the child's rights may have been violated?
→ Do they relate to any article(s) or protocol(s) in the Human Rights Act?
→ Do they relate to any other legal rights?
→ How can we now take this complaint forward?
→ What practical support can you offer? Is there any special language that could help our case?
→ Who should I contact to complain to?
→ How do I have to set out my complaint?
→ What arguments might the people I complain to come up with to stop me from getting the response I want?
→ Who should I contact to help me?

There are specific adult advocates (supporters) who could work with you through your issues and complaints. Details of how to contact them are in the following section.

Section 9 Useful contacts and further information

The organisations in this section are divided into the following:

→ Legal advice
→ Further information on human rights
→ Advice on specific issues
→ Other organisations.

There is a wide range of organisations providing advice and information. It is not possible to show them all here, but below is a selection.

Please note

The National Children's Bureau is not responsible for any advice or assistance provided by the listed organisations.

Legal advice

The Children's Legal Centre

The Children's Legal Centre is a national charity committed to promoting children's rights in the UK and worldwide. It is concerned with law and policy affecting children and young people.

Website: www.childrenslegalcentre.com

Phone:
Young People Freephone – 0800 783 2187
Child Law Advice Line – 0845 120 2948
Family Law Advice via Community Legal Advice –
0845 345 4345
General telephone – 01206 872466
All lines are open Monday–Friday, 9am–5pm

Email: clc@essex.ac.uk

Citizens Advice

Citizens Advice provides free, independent and confidential legal advice, and can help you find a solicitor.

Website: www.citizensadvice.org.uk

Phone: 020 7833 2181 to get details of your local CAB.

Community Legal Advice (formerly known as Community Legal Service Direct)

The website for Community Legal Advice has an online directory providing details of solicitors, advice agencies and information providers across England and Wales.

Website: www.clsdirect.org.uk

Phone helpline: 0845 345 4 345

Disability Law Service (DLS)

Disability Law Service provides high-quality information and advice to disabled and deaf people. As a national registered charity, DLS is independent, run by and for disabled people.

Website: www.dls.org.uk

Phone:
National advice line – 020 7791 9800
Minicom – 020 7791 9801
All lines are open Monday–Friday, 10am–1pm and 2pm–5pm

Email: advice@dls.org.uk

The Law Centres Federation

The Law Centres Federation is the voice of Law Centres, which provide free independent legal advice and representation to the most disadvantaged members of society.

Website: www.lawcentres.org.uk

Phone: 020 7428 4400

Email: info@lawcentres.org.uk

The Law Society

The Law Society has an online directory of law firms and solicitors. It does not provide legal advice but you can contact them for help in finding a lawyer.

Website: www.lawsociety.org.uk

Phone: 0870 606 6575

Email: info.services@lawsociety.org.uk

Further information on human rights

The **Human Rights Act** itself can be found at: www.opsi.gov.uk/acts/acts1998/19980042.htm or at www.bihr.org

The British Institute of Human Rights (BIHR)

BIHR is a human rights organisation that is committed to challenging inequality and injustice in everyday life here in the UK. It aims to achieve this by *bringing human rights to life* – supporting people to use human rights principles and standards to improve their own lives and as a tool for organisations to develop more effective public policy and practice.

It has developed some excellent information on human rights for: disabled people, older people, asylum seekers and in the area of mental health. It also has a 'human rights in schools' project which provides training, resources and whole-school guidelines to support human rights in schools. It is unable to provide advice to individuals.

Website: www.bihr.org

Children's Rights Alliance for England (CRAE)

CRAE exists to transform the lives and status of children in England by seeking the full implementation of the UN Convention on the Rights of the Child, EHRC and other human rights instruments. It wants all children to be respected as individual people and to be treated as full and equal members of society. In June 2008, CRAE launched the first ever national telephone and email advice service for children in England on equality and human rights.

Websites: www.crae.org.uk or www.getreadyforgeneva.org.uk

Phone:
General – 020 7278 8222
Confidential freephone* advice service –
0800 32 88 759 between 3.30 and 5.30pm, Tuesday to Thursday (* Standard charges apply from mobiles)

Email: info@crae.org.uk or advice@crae.org.uk for the advice service

Council of Europe (CoE)

The CoE has a new database of case law containing the decisions on cases relating to children's rights for the European Court of Human Rights. It can be found on their website.

Website: www.echr.coe.int

The Equality and Human Rights Commission

The new Commission brings together the work of the three previous equality commissions (gender, race and disability) and also takes on responsibility for age, sexual orientation, and religion or belief, as well as a broader human rights remit. It provides information and general advice and guidance.

Website: www.equalityhumanrights.com

Phone: 020 3117 0235

Email: info@equalityhumanrights.com

Liberty

Liberty works to promote human rights and protect civil liberties through a combination of test case litigation, lobbying, campaigning and the provision of free advice.

Liberty runs a free human rights advice service for members of the public. In the first instance you can go to their advice website, which contains a range of information on human rights issues and the UK Human Rights Act.

If you are unable to find the answer to your query on their website, you will find a query form on there which you can submit online or print out and post to 21 Tabard Street, London, SE1 4LA.

Websites: www.liberty-human-rights.org.uk or www.yourrights.org.uk

Phone (urgent queries): 0845 123 2307

Lines open Monday and Thursday 6.30pm–8.30pm, Wednesday 12.30pm–2.30pm

UNICEF

The United Nations Children's Fund (UNICEF) is an organisation that aims to raise awareness of the issues affecting children's everyday lives across the world. It is committed to ensuring that all the rights in the UNCRC are respected, and that every child can live a healthy life free from discrimination, poverty and abuse.

Websites: www.unicef.org and www.unicef.org.uk/youthvoice/rights.asp

Advice on specific issues

ARCH

ARCH (Action on Rights for Children) is an internet-based children's rights organisation.

Website: www.arch-ed.org

Phone: 020 8558 9317

Email: archrights@arch-ed.org

Asylum Aid

Asylum Aid is an independent, national charity. It works to secure protection for people seeking refuge in the United Kingdom from persecution and human rights abuses abroad.

Website: www.asylumaid.org.uk

Phone: 0207 354 9631

Email: info@asylumaid.org.uk

CAFCASS

CAFCASS looks after the interests of children involved in family proceedings, for example if their parents are going through a divorce.

Website: www.cafcass.gov.uk

Phone: 020 7510 7000

Dial UK

DIAL information and advice services are based throughout the UK and provide information and advice to disabled people and others on all aspects of living with a disability.

Website: www.dialuk.org.uk

Phone: (01302) 310 123

Email: informationenquiries@dialuk.org.uk

Family Rights Group

The Family Rights Group advises parents and other family members whose children are involved with or require social care services.

Website: www.frg.org.uk

Phone advice line: 0800 7311696

Opening hours: Monday–Friday 10am–12pm and 1.30pm–3.30pm

Immigration Advisory Service

The Immigration Advisory Service (IAS) is the UK's largest charity providing representation and advice on immigration and asylum law.

Website: www.iasuk.org

Joint Council for the Welfare of Immigrants

JCWI is an independent national voluntary organisation, campaigning for justice and combating racism in immigration and asylum law and policy.

Website: www.jcwi.org.uk

Phone: 020 7251 8708

Email: info@jcwi.org.uk

Just for Kids (Law)

Just for Kids provide advocates who act on behalf of young people in legal and quasi-legal proceedings. This includes advice and support in the areas of education, welfare, housing, mental and physical health, and substance misuse.

Website: www.justforkidslaw.org

Phone: 020 7266 7159

Email: info@justforkidslaw.org

JUSTICE

Through independent research, briefings and interventions, Justice seek to develop the law, influence public policy and promote human rights standards.

Website: www.justice.org.uk

Phone: 020 7329 5100

Email: admin@justice.org.uk

Mencap

Mencap is the UK's leading learning disability charity working with people with a learning disability and their families and carers.

Website: www.mencap.org.uk

Phone: 020 7454 0454

Email: information@mencap.org.uk

Mind

Mind is the leading mental health charity in England and Wales working to create a better life for everyone with experience of mental distress.

Website: www.mind.org.uk

Phone: 020 8519 2122

Email: contact@mind.org.uk

Refugee Council

The Refugee Council not only gives direct help and support but also works with asylum seekers and refugees to ensure their needs and concerns are addressed.

Website: www.refugeecouncil.org.uk

Phone: 020 7346 6700

The Refugee Legal Centre

The RLC provides legal advice and representation to those seeking protection under international and national human rights and asylum law.

Website: www.refugee-legal-centre.org.uk

Phone: 0207 780 3200; emergency line 07831 598057

Email: rlc@refugeelegalcentre.org.uk

Rethink

Rethink's aim is to make a practical and positive difference by providing hope and empowerment through effective services, information and support to all those experiencing severe mental health issues.

Website: www.rethink.org

Phone: (General enquiries) 0845 456 0455 or (National advice service) 0208 974 68 14

Lines open Monday, Wednesday and Friday 10am–3pm; Tuesday and Thursday, 10am–1pm

Email: info@rethink.org or advice@rethink.org

Shelter

Shelter helps those in need of a home to fight for their rights, get back on their feet, and find and keep a home.

Website: www.shelter.org.uk

Phone: 0845 458 4590 (for information) or 0808 800 4444 (for the housing advice helpline)

Email: info@shelter.org.uk

Stonewall

Stonewall works to achieve equality and justice for lesbians, gay men and bisexual people.

Website: www.stonewall.org.uk

Phone: 020 7593 1850

Email: info@stonewall.org.uk

Victim Support

Victim Support is the independent charity that helps people cope with the effects of crime. It provides free and confidential support to help people deal with their experience, whether or not they report the crime.

Website: www.victimsupport.org.uk

Victim support line: 0845 30 30 900

Lines are open:

9am–9pm Mondays to Fridays, 9am–7pm weekends, 9am–5pm bank holidays

Voice

Voice is one of the UK's leading voluntary organisations working and campaigning for children and young people in public care.

It works with children and young people looked after by the state, including those in children's homes, foster care, secure units and secure training centres, young offender institutions and unaccompanied asylum-seeking children and young people.

Website: www.voiceyp.org

Freephone number (for young people):
0808 800 5792

Lines open Monday–Friday, 9.30–5.30

WITNESS against abuse by health & care workers

WITNESS helps people who have been abused by health and social care workers; and works to prevent abuse.

Website: www.witnessagainstabuse.org.uk

Phone: 08454 500 300 (helpline), 020 7922 7799 (general)

Email: info@witnessagainstabuse.org.uk

Other organisations

Local Government Ombudsman

The LGO deals with complaints against local councils in England concerning a range of services including social services, housing and housing benefit. The LGO also deals with some complaints about education. The recommendations it gives are not legally binding but are usually upheld by local authorities.

Website: www.lgo.org.uk/contact.htm (general) or go direct to www.lgo.org.uk/young-people/index.htm (the young person section of the website)

Phone advice line: 0845 602 1983

Lines available Monday–Friday, 9am–4.45pm

Parliamentary and Health Service Ombudsman

The Ombudsman (of which there are several, 'Ombudspeople') looks into complaints that government departments, their agencies and some other public bodies in the UK – and the NHS in England – have not acted properly or fairly or have provided a poor service. You can submit your complaint by phone, email or via the website.

Website: www.ombudsman.org.uk/ or to make a complaint online go to www.ombudsman.org.uk/make_a_complaint/index.html

Phone: 0845 015 4033 (complaints helpline)

Lines open Monday–Friday, 8am–6pm

Email: phso.enquiries@ombudsman.org.uk

YoungMinds

YoungMinds is the UK's only national charity committed to improving the mental health and emotional well-being of all children and young people.

Website: www.youngminds.org.uk

Phone: 020 7336 8445

Participation Works

Participation Works enables organisations to involve young people effectively in the development, delivery and evaluation of the services that affect their lives. It is a consortium of six national children and young people's agencies made up of the British Youth Council, the Children's Rights Alliance for England, the National Children's Bureau, the National Council for Voluntary Youth Services, Save the Children, and The National Youth Agency.

Participation Works offers a comprehensive programme of activities and resources on participation – including workshops, training sessions and practitioner networks – designed to support organisations and practitioners that work with children and young people under 25 years old.

Website: www.participationworks.org.uk

Enquiry line: 0845 603 6725

Young NCB

This is NCB's free membership network for all children and young people aged under 18 and has over 350 members. Young NCB members speak out on issues they feel are important, such as children's rights, safety, sex and relationships, education, bullying, drugs, media and smacking.

Website: www.youngncb.org.uk

Phone: 020 7843 6099